People, Stupidity & Relationships

101 Quotes to Maintain Sanity

as told by Scott Evan Davis

a raz book production

ISBN: 979-8-9997041-0-8

Book design by Ranee A. Spina
Back Cover Photo Credit: Michael Kushner

Printed in the United States of America
First Paperback Edition April 2026

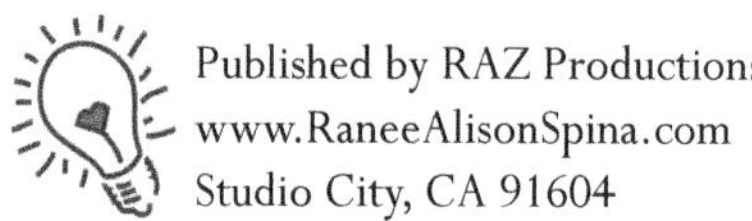

Published by RAZ Productions
www.RaneeAlisonSpina.com
Studio City, CA 91604

Scott,
Thank you for being the cute, charming, handsome face to such wonderful sarcasm – that's so close to my own sense of humor!
Ranee xox

Enjoy these quotes...
some from me,
some from memes,
and of course, some are classics.

I'm honored so many people
find joy in my sarcastic videos.
In challenging times,
it's important to have moments
that bring a smile to your face.

– Scott

People!

I don't know how anyone else feels,

but I hate when I go outside
and there are people...

#1

My therapist thinks I have a preoccupation with vengeance.

We'll see about that.

#2

One thing about me is that I never lose my patience.

I always know exactly where it is.

#3

I have friends that tell me I worry too much. But 97% of the things I worry about never happen,

so I think I know what I'm doing.

#4

Before I went to bed last night, I decided to sage my apartment to get rid of all the negative energy.

I woke up outside.

#5

Someone asked me if I was ready for the fall and I didn't quite know how to answer.

Then I realized, they didn't mean the collapse of society.

#6

Being on social media has taught me 2 important things:

1. There are a lot of brilliant people in the world.
2. They are vastly outnumbered.

#7

Have you ever had a conversation with someone,

and you couldn't tell if they were on too many drugs or not enough?

#8

Did you know? If you're naturally kind, you'll attract a lot of people...

that you don't like.

#9

There are so many people in this world who have inspired me...

to be nothing like them.

#10

My therapist told me I had generalized anxiety disorder.

I asked him if he could be more specific.

#11

Stop trying to be like everyone else.

Remember,
you don't like everyone else.

#12

There is only one thing I've ever regretted about burning bridges.

Some people weren't on them.

#13

Whenever someone tells me their kid is an angel,

I just think "awwww," so was Lucifer.

#14

Have you ever looked at someone and thought, "My heart has no room for you.

But my trunk does."

#15

Some days, it feels like you are surrounded by idiots.

And then other days,
you realize it's not just some days.

#16

There are two reasons why I don't trust people:

1. I don't know them.
2. I know them.

#17

Sorry, can you repeat that?

I couldn't hear you over the little voice in my head screaming, "Punch them in the throat."

#18

These days, one of the most important things to have with people is patience,

especially when there are too many witnesses.

#19

Listen,
if you can't laugh at yourself,

I'll do it.

#20

You really don't want to drive me crazy.

I'm close enough to walk.

#21

Someone once told me I should check my attitude. So, I did.

It's still there.

#22

I'm sorry, can you take a couple of steps back?

I'm allergic to nuts.

#23

I don't think we should have this conversation right now.

I'm out of the pills that make me like you.

#24

Here's a helpful strategy to help avoid stress whenever you have to go out in public:

Don't go.

#25

Don't you think the biggest problem in our society...

is all the people?

#26

Did you know? If you replace your coffee with green tea,

you will lose about 97% of what little joy you have left.

#27

Do you ever wish you could meet someone all over again for the very first time...

and run?

#28

I do appreciate your opinion,

but you look like someone
who buys condoms
on their way to a family reunion.

#29

When scientists finally discover what is at the center of the universe,

a lot of people are going to be disappointed that it isn't them.

#30

Some people play the victim so well,

they should carry around their own body chalk.

#31

The older I get, the more I understand...

why roosters start their day by screaming.

#32

I love it when people think...

they are punishing me
by not talking to me.

#33

When people tell me they are spiritual, I'm like,

"Demons are spirits, too, so be specific."

#34

People tell me I act like I don't care.

It's not an act.

#35

I don't want to interrupt you,

but you are about to exceed the limits of my medication.

#36

What do you look for when you meet someone for the first time?

For me, it's an exit.

#37

My biggest flaw:
When I ask someone
what their name is,

I forget to listen to
what their name is.

#38

My therapist told me I should sit down and write letters to all the people who have wronged me, and then burn them.

I said okay, but what do I do with the letters?

#39

Of course I would love to help you out...

Now which way did you come in?

#40

Stupidity!

It's very simple to be wise.

Just think of something stupid to say... then don't say it.

#41

Did you know that jellyfish have survived without brains for 650 million years?

That should bring hope to a lot of people.

#42

Two things: One, where have you been my whole life?

Two... would you please go back there?

#43

Did you know? Stupidity comes in all shapes and sizes -

and a lot of them look like people.

#44

It's a fact that stupidity is not a crime.

So, you're free to go.

#45

Don't be stupid.

There, I'm your life coach.

#46

Oh, don't be so paranoid. I'm not secretly judging you.

A lot of people know about it.

#47

It's clear you have a very open mind.

I can feel the draft from here.

#48

I don't think you're acting stupid.

I think it's the real thing.

#49

I don't know what makes you so stupid,

but it really works.

#50

No, no, I wasn't insulting you.

I was describing you.

#51

Give me a second.

It takes me time
to process so much stupidity
all at once.

#52

Can you repeat that? I was distracted.

I was trying to figure out how closely related your parents are.

#53

"You should always be yourself"

...is the worst advice you can give certain people.

#54

Everything happens for a reason.

Sometimes, that reason is you're stupid and make bad decisions.

#55

Before the internet, people thought stupidity was caused by lack of information.

Turns out... nope.

#56

You should never worry about what other people think.

They don't do it very often.

#57

Intelligence seems to follow you,

But you've always been faster.

#58

Sometimes I have to remember to just let the universe fix a problem.

Because if I fix it, I'm going to jail.

#59

I promise you, whatever you're about to say can wait...

until you're smarter.

#60

Is being stupid your profession,

or are you just gifted?

#61

Do you ever look at someone and wonder...

how they fit all that stupidity into one head?

#62

Of course I don't think you're worthless;

I can still use you as a bad example.

#63

If you're happy and you know it -

it's your meds.

#64

I didn't say you were stupid.

I said you ARE stupid.
It's not past tense.

#65

I guarantee the results of your IQ test...

were negative.

#66

We squint at the sun because it's bright.

We squint at people because they are not.

#67

They say we learn from our mistakes.

You must be brilliant.

#68

I wish I spoke idiot,

so I could tell you off
in your own language.

#69

I'm sorry,

were you born this stupid,
or did you train somewhere?

#70

Everyone has the right to be stupid.

Just don't abuse the privilege.

#71

I hate it when someone tells me to take one day at a time.

What else am I going to do?
Skip Tuesday?

#72

Relationships!

If you love someone, let them go.

If they come back to you, it's because no one else wanted them.

#73

No, I promise you. You're the only one I've ever been with...

all the rest were nines and tens.

#74

You know, I'll never forget the first time I met you.

But I'll keep trying.

#75

My idea of flirting is being as sarcastic as humanly possible,

and seeing if you can handle it.

#76

Did you know? If you lined up all your exes in a row,

you'd see a flow chart of your mental illness?

#77

It's important to remember, just because you haven't found the right person yet,

doesn't mean you will.

#78

Trust me, there is someone out there for everyone.

For you, it's a therapist.

#79

I’m the kind of person who will ask things I already know -

just to see if you’ll lie about it.

#80

They say opposites attract, so don't worry,

you'll meet someone intelligent.

#81

It's amazing how certain expressions completely change their meaning the older you get. For instance,

> *I saw my ex the other day and thought, "Wow... I'd hit that."*

#82

I've been asked,
"Why do you take an instant dislike towards people?"

And the answer is simple,
"It saves time."

#83

Every once in awhile someone will come along who will change your life for the better...

and sometimes that person is a bartender.

#84

Have you ever met someone and thought,

"I am so jealous of all the people that have never met you."

#85

Someone told me I was unapproachable.

So, I said, "And yet, here you are."

#86

Not to be awkward, but every time I am around you,

I have the strongest desire to be alone.

#87

Now that we've met, I can absolutely see myself spending the rest of my life...

avoiding you.

#88

Have you ever read a text, and thought to yourself, "Wow... what a psychopath,"

and then hit send?

#89

Stop thinking you need a relationship to be happy. You don't.

You need money.

#90

The first thing I notice when someone comes up to talk to me...

is the audacity.

#91

If I promise to miss you,

will you go away?

#92

Life is not a fairy tale.

If you lose your shoe at midnight,
you're drunk.

#93

Stop worrying if other people like you.

They don't.

#94

Remember, the first step to forgiveness is realizing...

the other person was born an idiot.

#95

There are two sides to every story,

but I'm right on both.

#96

I am so tired of the "kill em with kindness" approach.

It's taking way longer than expected.

#97

Being in a relationship means solving problems together.

(Problems you would not have if you were single.)

#98

My ex has three spirit animals.

Lion, ass, cheetah.

#99

I think my problem is...

I tend to see
how red the flag can get.

#100

This is just a friendly reminder:
If you want flowers on Valentine's Day,

you should plant them now.

#101

How It All Started

Like many questionable life choices, this one began during the pandemic. With too much time, too many thoughts, and absolutely nowhere to go, I started posting short videos on social media.

No grand plan. No strategy. Just one-liners. Observations.

I wanted to make people laugh - the kind of sarcastic thoughts you usually keep to yourself or text to a friend who gets you.

Turns out, I have a knack for sarcasm. People started responding, then following, then sharing. Somewhere along the way, these quick, throwaway lines became the thing I was known for, and the comments kept coming:

"Please put these in a book."
"I need all of these in one place."
"This is exactly how my brain works."

So here we are.
This book is essentially a greatest hits album of my favorite sarcastic quotes. People asked. I finally listened. Now give it a read, memorize some if you like... and go get em.

-SED

Connect

www.ScottEvanDavis.com
Social Platforms: @scottevandavis
LinkedIn: Scott Evan Davis

About Scott

Scott Evan Davis is an award-winning writer, composer, teacher and professional overthinker.

* Courage of Theatre Award for *POWERFUL DAY*, a musical written with autistic children.
* *If the World Only Knew* (composer/lyricist) is sung globally as an anthem for autism.
* MAC Award for Best Song *Before I Forget*, about dementia.
* *New Yorker of the Week* recipient for work with Epic Players, a NYC neurodiverse theatre company.
* Original musical *INDIGO* UK Premiere in 2025.
* Children's book *Queen Bea* March 2026.

Professional Training:
Emerson College
Acadamy of Music and Dramatic Arts (AMDA)

Acknowledgements

Thank you to everyone who has watched, shared, stitched, commented, and sent my videos to their group chats with the caption, "This is you."

Thank you to my friends, who have spent years rolling their eyes.

And finally, thank you to The Golden Girls, who taught me at a very young age that impeccable timing, and a well-placed pause, could stop people cold. I've been chasing that level of sarcasm ever since.

www.ingramcontent.com/pod-product-compliance
Ingram Content Group UK Ltd.
Pitfield, Milton Keynes, MK11 3LW, UK
UKHW062253290726
14090UKWH00017B/666

9 798999 704108